Thanks for making Orinda feel like home.

Tom & Tricia

THIS BOOK
BELONGS TO:

Barbara & Vaughn Simon

12/25/93

DATE

Christmas Memories

Of
all the
holidays,
Christmas is
the one that brings
family and friends to-
gether the most. It is a
time when the mention of
Grandma's sugar cookies or
the smell of turkey cooking can
set your mouth to watering. A time
when the sound of jingle bells jingling
or Christmas carols pealing from the church
tower can create the wonder of this season of
love. The feelings of the season come in all shapes
and sizes, from the feeling of snow flakes or Jack Frost
nipping at your nose to the feelings of love, hope and good
will to all men. In a hundred languages, in a thousand different
traditions, the meaning of Christmas unites the world in joyful celebration of the birth of baby Jesus around the creche, the ceppo, the bonfire,
or the Christmas tree.
It is a time to wonder.
It is a time to ponder.
It is a time to remember.

Memories need a place to rest between the tellings, lest we forget Christmas Past.
Keep your remembrances of the love of family, the joy of friends and the warmth of
good times. But more than just a place to store your memories, we hope this
Christmas album will become part of your celebration of the joyous season-to-come
as each year you read the stories, songs and poems which tell the
traditions of Christmas and instill us with its Spirit.

1

The First Christmas

And it came to pass in those days that a decree went out
from Caesar Augustus that all the world should be registered.
This census first took place while Quirinius was governing Syria. So all
went to be registered, everyone to his own city. And Joseph also went up
from Galilee, out of the city of Nazareth, into Judea, to the city of David,
which is called Bethlehem, because he was of the house and lineage of David,
to be registered with Mary, his betrothed wife, who was with child. So it was,
that while they were there, the days were completed for her to be delivered.
And she brought forth her firstborn Son, and wrapped Him in swaddling
cloths, and laid Him in a manger, because there was no room for them in the inn.
Now there were in the same country shepherds living out in the fields, keeping
watch over their flock by night. And behold, an angel of the Lord stood before
them, and the glory of the Lord shone around them, and they were greatly afraid.
Then the angel said to them, "Do not be afraid, for behold, I bring you good
tidings of great joy which will be to all people. "For there is born to you this day in
the city of David a Savior, who is Christ the Lord."And this will be the sign to you:
You will find a Babe wrapped in swaddling cloths, lying in a manger." And suddenly
there was with the angel a multitude of the heavenly host praising God and saying:
"Glory to God in the highest,
And on earth peace,
good will toward men!"

So it was, when the angels had gone away from them into heaven,
that the shepherds said to one another, "Let us now go to Bethlehem and see
this thing that has come to pass, which the Lord has made known to us."And they
came with haste and found Mary and Joseph, and the Babe lying in a manger. Now
when they had seen Him, they made widely known the saying which was told them
concerning this Child. And all those who heard it marveled at those things which
were told them by the shepherds. But Mary kept all these things and pondered them
in her heart. Then the shepherds returned, glorifying and praising the things that
they had heard and seen, as it was told them.
Luke 2:1-20 NKJV

The Trees of Christmas

O Tannenbaum"

O Christmas tree,

O Christmas tree,

How lovely are your branches.

In summer sun, in winter snow,

A dress of green you always show.

O Christmas tree,

O Christmas tree,

How lovely are your branches.

O Christmas tree,

O Christmas tree,

With happiness we greet you.

When decked with candles once a year,

You fill our hearts with yuletide cheer.

O Christmas tree,

O Christmas tree,

With happiness we greet you.

The evergreen tree has always held the promise of the return of life to all that seemed brown and dead in the rest of nature. The ritual of cutting branches of the evergreen tree or whole trees and taking them inside in the month of the shortest days in the year go back long before the first Christmas. Evergreens were the symbol that life would continue.

St. Boniface was a Christian missionary around the eighth century. In his efforts to win the Germans over to a worship of Christ, he is said to have pointed to a tiny fir tree as a symbol of Christ as the bringer of life "ever green," tying together the ritual of the evergreen tree and Christianity forever.

THE TREE THAT BLOOMED AT CHRISTMAS

Legends of trees that blossomed in the dead of winter, at Christmastime, helped convert the evergreen tree into a Christian symbol. The most famous of these is the Glastonbury thorn tree which grew from the staff of Joseph of Arimathea where he planted it around 70 A. D., when bringing the gospel to England. Each year thereafter it would bloom at Christmas.

If a miracle tree did not occur in a town, a representation was easily made by fastening handmade flowers to a tree. A merchant's guild in Riga, Latvia, was the first recorded incidence of such a practice in 1510. Soon the custom spread from flowers to other things. By the seventeenth century, the German tree, called Christbaum, the "Christ tree" provided food for body and spirit with beautifully shaped, elaborate candies and cookies for the tree.

AND THE TREE WAS LIGHTED

The story is told that, while looking through the branches of a tree at a clear and starry sky one Christmas Eve in the sixteenth century, Martin Luther was inspired to put candles on the Christmas tree. The candles were to symbolize the Christ Child as the Light of the world.

Three hundred years after Martin Luther and only three years after Thomas Alva Edison had demonstrated his electric light bulb in 1879, the first custom-made string of eighty little colored bulbs were made for the Christmas tree in the New York mansion of Edward H. Johnson, the vice-president of the Edison Electric Company. Only the wealthy were able to afford electric Christmas lights for many years, but in 1903, more than twenty years later, General Electric and the Ever-Ready Company collaborated to make a ready-made string of Christmas lights. Although more in the reach of the average man at twelve dollars a set, the lights were still approximately a week's wages for the average working man.

The Red and Green Of Christmas

MISTLETOE

The mistletoe, by myth and legend, was made a symbol of love with the promise to bestow a kiss on all who pass beneath it by Frigga, mother of Balder, the best loved of all the Norse Gods. A dart of mistletoe, thrown by Balder's own blind brother at the urging and direction of the jealous trickster Loki, killed Balder. Although heavily grieved, Frigga forgave the innocent plant and made it the symbol of love.

According to an old English custom, a man had to pluck a berry from the mistletoe branch for each girl he kissed until he ran out of girls to be kissed or the branch was bare.

Ancient ceremonies of kissing beneath the mistletoe symbolized the ending of old grievances.

MYTHS OF HOLLY

In England, the prickly holly is referred to as "he," and the non-prickly holly as "she." An old tradition has it that whichever kind of holly is first brought into the house at Christmas determines who will rule the house for the new year.

A sprig of holly on one's bedpost will bring pleasant dreams.

Holly hung in the home assures the occupants of good luck.

THE POINSETTIA

In some legends of Mexico it is a little boy who prayed at the altar on Christmas Eve because he was so poor he had no gift to bring the Christ Child on his birthday. The first flame-bright "Flor de la Noche Buena," Flower of the Holy Night, sprang at his feet as his miracle gift to give. In other legends it is the story of a young girl who had no gift to bring and as she lay weeping in the cathedral, an angel appeared and told her to pick some tall weeds growing nearby. When she placed them on the altar as her offering to the baby Jesus, they burst into the brilliant red flower.

It was Dr. Joel Roberts Poinsett, an amateur botanist and American ambassador to Mexico from 1825 to 1829 who brought the beautiful red and green plant back to his home in South Carolina where he propagated cuttings across the country. The plant was eventually named after him.

The bright red petals of the poinsettia are really the leaves. The tiny red and gold blossoms that lie in the middle are the flower.

Old English Ballad

The mistletoe bough
On the festive throng
Looks down,
Amid echoes of mirthful song...
And who is she
That will not allow
A kiss claimed
Under the mistletoe bough?

An Old Carol

The holly's up,
The house is all bright,
The tree is ready,
The candles alight;
Rejoice and be glad,
All children tonight.

A Yule Log Prayer

May the fire of this log
warm the cold;
May the hungry be fed;
May the weary find rest,
and may all enjoy Heaven's peace.

Traditional prayer said when
the yule log is lighted.

Christmas Traditions

CHRISTMAS CARDS

The custom of giving Christmas cards began in the 1800's. English schoolchildren away from home created elaborate handmade pieces with their best penmanship to display their progress in school and perhaps remind their parents that the gift-giving season was soon at hand. The advent of the printing press and the penny post in England brought about the wholesale entry of the custom of sending Christmas Cards.

THE CHRISTMAS CANDLE

It is according to legend that candles in the window are to guide the Christ Child as he wanders from house to house on Christmas Eve.

THE YULE LOG

The English custom was to burn the Yule log on Christmas Eve, but centuries ago the Scandinavians believed the sun was attached to a big wheel which stopped for twelve days during the winter solstice. It was up to them to keep the fire going for that period of time.

The ritual of the Yule log was the center of much singing and merriment from beginning to end. It was thought to be good luck to sit on the Yule log before it was burned; and bad luck if the fire went out quickly. The Yule log had to be lighted from a piece of last year's log.

HANGING THE STOCKING

An elderly nobleman, friend of the parents of Nicholas (later to become St. Nicholas), had sadly lost all of his wealth. His three lovely daughters could no longer be wed as they had not the required dowry. It was decided in a choice of lots that one of the daughters would sell herself into slavery to provide dowries for her sisters. Nicholas, hearing of the plight of the three daughters, waited only for night to fall. Under cover of darkness he went to the home of the nobleman where he dropped a small bag of gold down the chimney. It fell into the eldest daughter's stocking which was hanging there to dry. Shortly after, the eldest daughter was married. Two times more Nicholas visited the house in secret and left gold for the two other daughters who were likewise married. The traditional orange in the toe of the stocking today symbolizes the gold St. Nicholas left.

Christmas Traditions

Merrie Christmas

THE CHRISTMAS CAROL

St. Francis of Assisi in 1223 was the first to create a life-sized Nativity scene or "creche" where he and others sang the first Christmas carols. The word "carol" has its origin in the circular folk dances ("ring dances") that were a part of the custom of the carol throughout Italy, France, England, Germany and Spain.

Silent Night

This most beloved Christmas carol was written by Father Josef Mohr, assistant priest at St. Nicholas' church at Oberndorf, Austria, on Christmas Eve, 1818. With the organ for the church unable to be played, Father Josef wrote the three six-line stanzas of poetry and asked the church organist Franz Gruber to set it to music for a choir and guitar accompaniment. Since Gruber was not as proficient on the guitar as he was on the organ, the melody was very simple. Father Mohr never heard the "Song from Heaven" as it was called as it gained popularity around the world. He died in 1848 and was buried on St. Nicholas' day.

> Silent night, holy night,
> All is calm, all is bright
> Round yon Virgin Mother and Child!
> Holy Infant so tender and mild,
> Sleep in heavenly peace.
>
> Silent night, holy night,
> Shepherds quake at the sight,
> Glories stream from heaven afar,
> Heavenly hosts sing alleluia;
> Christ, the Saviour, is born.
>
> Silent night, holy night,
> Son of God, love's pure light
> Radiant beams from Thy holy face,
> With the dawn of redeeming grace,
> Jesus, Lord, at Thy birth.

A Christmas Prayer

Little Jesus, wast Thou shy
Once, and just so small as I?
And what did it feel like to be
Out of Heaven, and just like me?

Hadst Thou ever any toys,
Like us little girls and boys? And didst
Thou play in Heaven with all The
angels that were not too tall, With stars
for marbles? Did the things Play Can
you see me? through their wings?

Didst Thou kneel at night to pray,
And didst Thou join Thy hands,
this way? And dost Thou like it best,
that we Should join our hands to pray
to Thee? I used to think, before I knew,
The prayer not said unless we do.

And did Thy Mother at the night
Kiss Thee, and fold the clothes in right?
And didst Thou feel quite good in bed,
Kissed, and sweet, and Thy prayers said?

Thou canst not have forgotten all
That it feels like to be small.
To Thy Father show my prayer
(He will look, Thou art so fair),
And say: "O Father, I, Thy Son,
Bring the prayer of a little one."

And He will smile, that children's tongue
Has not changed since Thou wast young!

—Francis Thompson
(1859-1907)

7

Christmas

Jolly Old St. Nicholas

Old song

Jolly old St. Nicholas
      Bend your ear this way
Don't you tell a single soul
      What I'm going to say.

Christmas Eve is coming soon;
      Now you dear old man,
Whisper what you'll bring to me;
      Tell me if you can."

The origin of our beneficient and gift-giving Saint Nicholas or Santa Claus comes from the stories told of Nicholas, the youthful Bishop of Myra in Asia Minor, who later became St. Nicholas for his charitable acts to the poor and the miracles attributed to his legend some 1700 years ago. The gift-giver can be either a man or a woman, tiny or hearty, can ride a camel or fly through the air, and can distribute gifts on Christmas or Epiphany, but the sentiment is all the same. Although he is St. Nicholas to much of the world, he is also known as Sinter Klass to the Dutch, Papa Noel in Brazil; Kristkindl, the Christ Child, which became Kriss Kringle, to the German culture; Father Christmas to the English, including Australia and New Zealand; and Petit Noel or Pere Noel to the French. In Russia he was first called The Miracle Maker, then changed to Grandfather Frost. The Japanese Hoteiosho is said to have eyes in the back of his head as well as the front—all the better to watch the behavior of little boys and girls—and the Chinese are visited by Lam Khoong-Khoong or Dun Che Lao Ren, the Christmas Old Man, who fills their stockings. La Befana is the female form of Santa Claus in Italy, while the more diminutive, bearded Tomten are the gift-bringers in Sweden, and the even tinier Jule Nissen bring gifts to the people of Norway and Denmark.

Yes, Virginia, There Is a Santa Claus

Dear Editor:

    I am 8 years old.

Some of my little friends say

    there is no Santa Claus. Papa says, "

    If you see it in The Sun it's so." Please tell me the truth;

        is there a Santa Claus?

            Virginia O'Hanlon,

            115 West 95th Street

Francis P. Church was a veteran newspaperman and had been with The Sun for twenty years when he was assigned the task of answering this young reader's timeless question. His reply became perhaps the most famous newspaper editorial of all time.

Virginia, your little friends are wrong. They have been affected by the skepticism of a skeptical age. They do not believe except they see. They think that nothing can be which is not comprehensible by their little minds. All minds, Virginia, whether they be men's or children's, are little. In this great universe of ours man is a mere insect, an ant, in his intellect, as compared with the boundless world about him, as measured by the intelligence capable of grasping the whole of truth and knowledge.

    Yes, Virginia, there is a Santa Claus. He exists as certainly as love and generosity and devotion exist, and you know that they abound and give to your life its highest beauty and joy. Alas! how dreary would be the world if there were no Santa Claus! It would be as dreary as if there were no Virginias. There would be no childlike faith then, no poetry, no romance to make tolerable this existence. We should have no enjoyment, except in sense and sight. The eternal light with which childhood fills the world would be extinguished.

    Not believe in Santa Claus! You might as well not believe in fairies! You might get your papa to hire men to watch in all the chimneys on Christmas Eve to catch Santa Claus, but even if they did not see Santa Claus coming down, what would that prove? Nobody sees Santa Claus, but that is no sign that there is no Santa Claus. The most real things in the world are those that neither children nor men can see.

    No Santa Claus! Thank God, he lives, and he lives forever. A thousand years from now, Virginia, nay, ten times ten thousand years from now, he will continue to make glad the heart of childhood.

        —by Francis. P. Church for The New York Sun,

September 21, 1897

A Visit From St. Nicholas

"Twas the night before Christmas, when all through the house
Not a creature was stirring, not even a mouse;
The stockings were hung by the chimney with care,
In hopes that St. Nicholas soon would be there;
The children were nestled all snug in their beds,
While visions of sugar-plums danced in their heads;
And mama in her kerchief and I in my cap
Had just settled our brains for a long winter's nap,
When out on the lawn there arose such a clatter,
I sprang from my bed to see what was the matter.
Away to the window I flew like a flash,
Tore open the shutters, and threw up the sash;
The moon, on the breast of the new-fallen snow,
Gave a lustre of midday to objects below;
When what to my wondering eyes should appear
But a miniature sleigh and eight tiny reindeer,
With a little old driver, so lively and quick,
I knew in a moment, it must be St. Nick.
More rapid than eagles his coursers they came,
And he whistled and shouted and called them by name:
"Now Dasher! now Dancer! now Prancer! now Vixen!
On, Comet! on, Cupid! on Donder and blitzen!
To the top of the porch! To the top of the wall!
Now, dash away, dash away, dash away, all!"
As dry leaves that before the wild hurricane fly,
When they meet with an obstacle, mount to the sky,
So up to the housetop the coursers they flew,
With the sleigh full of toys and St. Nicholas too.

And then, in a twinkling, I heard on the roof
The prancing and pawing of each little hoof.
As I drew in my head and was turning around,
Down the chimney St. Nicholas came with a bound.
He was dressed all in fur, from his head to his foot,
And his clothes were all tarnished with ashes and soot;
A bundle of toys he had flung on his back,
And he looked like a peddler just opening his pack.
His eyes: how they twinkled! his dimples: how merry!
His cheeks were like roses, his nose like a cherry;
His droll little mouth was drawn up like a bow,
And the beard on his chin was as white as the snow.
The stump of a pipe he held tight in his teeth,
And the smoke, it encircled his head like a wreath:
He had a broad face, and a little round belly,
That shook, when he laughed, like a bowl full of jelly;
He was chubby and plump, a right jolly old elf;
And I laughed, when I saw him, in spite of myself,
A wink of his eye and a twist of his head
Soon gave me to know I had nothing to dread.
He spoke not a word, but went straight to his work,
And filled all the stockings; then turned with a jerk,
And laying his finger aside of his nose,
And giving a nod, up the chimney he rose.
He sprang to his sleigh, to his team gave a whistle,
And away they all flew like the down of a thistle;
But I heard him exclaim, ere he drove out of sight,
"Happy Christmas to all, and to all a good-night!"

As a professor at a theological seminary, Clement Clarke Moore was a distinguished scholar, author of classical uerse and publisher of sermons. A Visit from St Nicholas was written as a "little nothing" he composed for his children's Christmas and read to them on December 23, 1822. A guest heard the recitation, copied down the poem, and the following Christmas sent it anonymously to the Troy Snottoel (New York) which published it with a note of thanks to the unknown author. Although Moore felt the poem beneath the dignity of his usual work, he finally acknowledged his authorship in 1844 and allowed the poem to appear in his collected works.

Wassail

Wassailing brings to mind the wassail bowl, a potent punch, merry people and singing. The wassail mixture itself is a recipe of wines, sugar, eggs and roasted apples specially concocted and protected by the manor of the house himself. The word wassail comes from an Anglo-Saxon term, waes hael, which means "be in good health," "be well" or "hale." The custom of wassailing began as a ritual salute to the apple tree to ensure a successful and increasing yield the next year. Festive people, rather in the way of a procession during the twelve days of Christmas, would visit the major trees in an orchard and sprinkle wassail on the roots or "christen" the tree trunk with a bottle of the wassail mixture. The tree would be heralded with songs, toasts, or recitations for a good season. The people would make loud noises as part of the ritual to scare off evil spirits and partly as an excuse for loud merriment. The group would proceed from tree to tree, eventually ending up as a caroling group going from house to house and being invited in for punch. Over the centuries, the wassail bowl has become a punch bowl and remains indoors, and the procession of carolers now go from door to door rather than from tree to tree.

A CHRISTMAS TOAST

"Lamb's Wool" was the ceremonial hot drink filling the wassail bowls of merry old England. It was made of the traditional wassail ingredients of hot ale, eggs, sugar, spices, and roasted apples, and got its name from the "toast" floating on top which made it look like lamb's wool. "Lamb's Wool" with its "toast" is the origin of the drinking "toast" —to drink to the well-being of another.

The Wassail Brew

A Recipe

Bake one dozen apples in the oven.
Keep hot.
Boil 1 cup water while adding a pinch of
nutmeg and mace, three cloves,
1/2 teaspoon of powdered allspice,
1 teaspoon powdered ginger,
1 stick of cinnamon about 2 inches long.
Remove from heat, then boil again.
Place four quarts of apple cider in a
large pan over low heat
and add the spiced water mixture.
Separate one dozen eggs and beat whites and yolks
separately first, then mix together.
Place the egg mixture in a large punch bowl
and slowly pour in the heated cider
while beating constantly to maintain
the frothy consistency.
Add the hot apples.
    Makes 24 cups.

JINGLE BELLS! JINGLE BELLS! JINGLE ALL THE WAY! OH,WHAT FUN IT IS TO RIDE IN A

ONE-HORSE OPEN SLEIGH! • JINGLE BELLS! JINGLE BELLS! JINGLE ALL THE WAY! OH, WHAT FUN IT IS TO RIDE IN A

ONE-HORSE OPEN SLEIGH! • JINGLE BELLS! JINGLE BELLS! JINGLE ALL THE WAY! OH, WHAT

FUN IT IS TO RIDE IN A ONE-HORSE OPEN SLEIGH! • JINGLE BELLS! JINGLE BELLS! JINGLE ALL THE WAY! OH, WHAT

Favorite Family Recipes

Favorite Family Recipes

Favorite Family Recipes

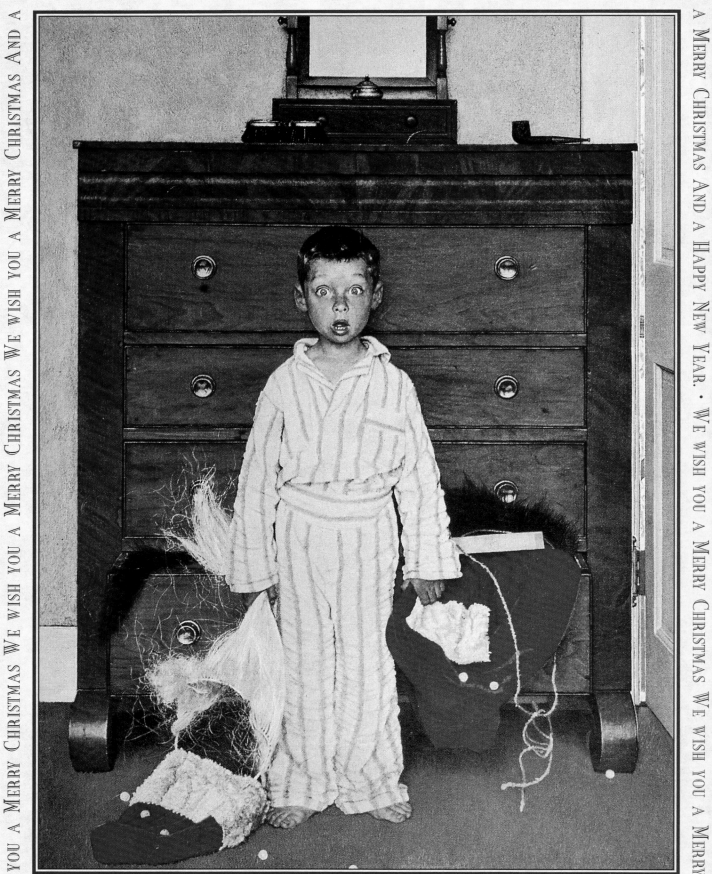

Memories of this past year

— 1993 —

(Place photo here)

Inscription _____

(Place photo here)

Inscription _____

1993

Anne Christmas Lunch

Veggies + Dill Dip + Crackers
Spinach Ball   Mixed Nuts
Cheese Squares

Champagne

Mixed Green Salad / Raspberry Vinaigrette
Feta Cheese + Toasted Walnuts

Christmas Eve and other special events of the season

We celebrated Christmas Day

Biggest surprise of the season

Seasons Greetings

(place Christmas Card here)

WE EXCHANGED GREETINGS WITH OUR FRIENDS

Name	Sent / Rec'd	Name	Sent / Rec'd
	☐ ☐		☐ ☐
	☐ ☐		☐ ☐
	☐ ☐		☐ ☐
	☐ ☐		☐ ☐
	☐ ☐		☐ ☐
	☐ ☐		☐ ☐
	☐ ☐		☐ ☐
	☐ ☐		☐ ☐
	☐ ☐		☐ ☐
	☐ ☐		☐ ☐
	☐ ☐		☐ ☐
	☐ ☐		☐ ☐
	☐ ☐		☐ ☐
	☐ ☐		☐ ☐
	☐ ☐		☐ ☐
	☐ ☐		☐ ☐

Gifts

_____
_____
_____
_____
_____
_____
_____
_____
_____

Special Guests of the Season

Special Decorations, Trips, Treats, and Menus

Memories of this past year
- 1994 -

(Place photo here)

Inscription _____

(Place photo here)

Inscription _____

Christmas Eve and other special events of the season

Norman Rockwell

We celebrated Christmas Day

Biggest surprise of the season

Seasons Greetings

(place Christmas Card here)

WE EXCHANGED GREETINGS WITH OUR FRIENDS

Name	Sent / Rec'd	Name	Sent / Rec'd
_____	☐ ☐	_____	☐ ☐
_____	☐ ☐	_____	☐ ☐
_____	☐ ☐	_____	☐ ☐
_____	☐ ☐	_____	☐ ☐
_____	☐ ☐	_____	☐ ☐
_____	☐ ☐	_____	☐ ☐
_____	☐ ☐	_____	☐ ☐
_____	☐ ☐	_____	☐ ☐
_____	☐ ☐	_____	☐ ☐
_____	☐ ☐	_____	☐ ☐
_____	☐ ☐	_____	☐ ☐
_____	☐ ☐	_____	☐ ☐
_____	☐ ☐	_____	☐ ☐
_____	☐ ☐	_____	☐ ☐
_____	☐ ☐	_____	☐ ☐
_____	☐ ☐	_____	☐ ☐

Gifts

TO REMEMBER   FROM THE HEART

_____   _____
_____   _____
_____   _____
_____   _____
_____   _____
_____   _____
_____   _____
_____   _____

Special Guests of the Season

Special Decorations, Trips, Treats, and Menus

Memories of this past year
-1995-

(Place photo here)

Inscription _____

(Place photo here)

Inscription _____

Christmas Eve and other special events of the season

We celebrated Christmas Day

Biggest surprise of the season

Seasons Greetings

(place Christmas Card here)

WE EXCHANGED GREETINGS WITH OUR FRIENDS

Name	Sent / Rec'd	Name	Sent / Rec'd
	☐ ☐		☐ ☐
	☐ ☐		☐ ☐
	☐ ☐		☐ ☐
	☐ ☐		☐ ☐
	☐ ☐		☐ ☐
	☐ ☐		☐ ☐
	☐ ☐		☐ ☐
	☐ ☐		☐ ☐
	☐ ☐		☐ ☐
	☐ ☐		☐ ☐
	☐ ☐		☐ ☐
	☐ ☐		☐ ☐
	☐ ☐		☐ ☐
	☐ ☐		☐ ☐
	☐ ☐		☐ ☐
	☐ ☐		☐ ☐
	☐ ☐		☐ ☐

Gifts

_____   _____
_____   _____
_____   _____
_____   _____
_____   _____
_____   _____
_____   _____
_____   _____
_____   _____

Special Guests of the Season

Special Decorations, Trips, Treats, and Menus

Memories of this past year
— 1996 —

(Place photo here)

Inscription _____

(Place photo here)

Inscription _____

Christmas Eve and other special events of the season

We celebrated Christmas Day

Biggest surprise of the season

Seasons Greetings

(place Christmas Card here)

WE EXCHANGED GREETINGS WITH OUR FRIENDS

Name	Sent / Rec'd	Name	Sent / Rec'd
_____	☐ ☐	_____	☐ ☐
_____	☐ ☐	_____	☐ ☐
_____	☐ ☐	_____	☐ ☐
_____	☐ ☐	_____	☐ ☐
_____	☐ ☐	_____	☐ ☐
_____	☐ ☐	_____	☐ ☐
_____	☐ ☐	_____	☐ ☐
_____	☐ ☐	_____	☐ ☐
_____	☐ ☐	_____	☐ ☐
_____	☐ ☐	_____	☐ ☐
_____	☐ ☐	_____	☐ ☐
_____	☐ ☐	_____	☐ ☐
_____	☐ ☐	_____	☐ ☐
_____	☐ ☐	_____	☐ ☐
_____	☐ ☐	_____	☐ ☐
_____	☐ ☐	_____	☐ ☐

Gifts

_____   _____
_____   _____
_____   _____
_____   _____
_____   _____
_____   _____
_____   _____
_____   _____
_____   _____

Special Guests of the Season

Special Decorations, Trips, Treats, and Menus

Memories of this past year

(Place photo here)

Inscription _____

(Place photo here)

Inscription _____

Christmas Eve and other special events of the season

We celebrated Christmas Day

Biggest surprise of the season

Seasons Greetings

(place Christmas Card here)

WE EXCHANGED GREETINGS WITH OUR FRIENDS

Name	Sent / Rec'd	Name	Sent / Rec'd
	❑ ❑		❑ ❑
	❑ ❑		❑ ❑
	❑ ❑		❑ ❑
	❑ ❑		❑ ❑
	❑ ❑		❑ ❑
	❑ ❑		❑ ❑
	❑ ❑		❑ ❑
	❑ ❑		❑ ❑
	❑ ❑		❑ ❑
	❑ ❑		❑ ❑
	❑ ❑		❑ ❑
	❑ ❑		❑ ❑
	❑ ❑		❑ ❑
	❑ ❑		❑ ❑
	❑ ❑		❑ ❑
	❑ ❑		❑ ❑
	❑ ❑		❑ ❑

Gifts

To Remember

From the Heart

_____
_____
_____
_____
_____
_____
_____
_____
_____
_____

Special Guests of the Season

Special Decorations, Trips, Treats, and Menus